Grandparents are Special

A 600-Word-Level Reader

Allyson Rothburd

Illustrated by Conrad Malatak

Pro Lingua Associates

Pro Lingua Associates, Publishers
20 Elm Street
Brattleboro, Vermont 05301 USA

Office: 802 257 7779
Orders: 800 366 4775
www.ProLinguaAssociates.com
E-mail: prolingu@sover.net
SAN: 216-0579

This book was designed and set in Palatino type by Arthur A. Burrows. It was printed and bound by Worzalla Printers in Stevens Point, Wisconsin.

The illustrations are by Conrad Malatak and Harriet Spivack

Printed in the United States of America
First printing 1999. 3000 copies.

Acknowledgments

Thanks to some very special people

A very special thank you to **Conrad Malatak**, my neighbor and principal illustrator of the book, who through his talent, creativity and kindness helped make this project come true.

Due to an unfortunate accident, Conrad was unable to complete all the illustrations. My dear colleague and fine artist, **Harriet Spivack**, had the difficult task of completing Conrad's work. Thank you, Harriet, for a fine job.

To my special crew at home, a loving thank you to my husband, **Dr. Jeffrey Rothburd** for all his support in everything I do (except my cooking.)

Thanks to our daughter **Adrienne Rothburd**, who never put me through the "terrible twos" or "trying teens." You're a kind, thoughtful, beautiful college student whom I am very proud of and admire.

To my mother **Edythe Roth** — thank you for everything and for still telling me I should get more sleep.

To **Eva Roberts**, who taught me above and beyond my violin lessons and became a dear friend who will always have a special place in my heart.

To **Chris Franchina**, who bails me out with her computer when I'm not behind mine.

To **my colleagues and dear friends (109)** whom I've learned so much from over the years of working together.

To **Raymond Clark** and **Arthur Burrows** at Pro Lingua Associates for your trust in me and for making this whole experience run smoothly.

Lastly, I'd like to acknowledge the fact that I have the pleasure of not only teaching **my students** every day, but of learning from them as well.

Thank you all.

Dedication

In memory of

My grandparents — Harry and Fannie Charnow

My father — Max Roth

My sister — Brenda Sternbaum

And to all the people who have made an impact on someone by being
Very Special

Grandparents are special. They listen to you. They love you. They make you feel good.

My friends have grandparents. Kumiko's grandparents are from Japan. They speak Japanese. Miguel's grandparents are from Mexico. They speak Spanish. Marcia's grandparents are from Brazil. They speak Portuguese. Fougere's grandparents are from Haiti. They speak French. My grandparents are from Russia. They speak Russian.

Portuguese Mexican Russian French Japanese

3

My name is Olga. I live with my mom and dad. They work in offices in the same big building. They leave for work at eight o'clock in the morning. Before they leave we have breakfast together at seven o'clock. Mom makes hot cereal for me every day. I like her hot cereal a lot. I also drink orange juice, and sometimes I eat some toast from my Dad's plate. After breakfast, they kiss me goodbye. "See you tonight," they say. I lock the door when I leave for school.

My grandparents are very helpful. Every day I stay with them after school. My mom and dad come home from work at six o'clock in the evening. They come for me at my grandparents' house.

My school is five blocks from my house. I walk to school. Sometimes I walk by myself. Other times I walk with my friends Kumiko, Miguel, Marcia, and Fougere. We are in the fifth grade. We are learning English.

I like walking to school, especially in the spring. I walk by a house with a big garden. I smell the flowers. I love the different colors of the flowers. Some are yellow and orange and purple. Some are red. Some are blue. The grass is very green. Walking to school in the spring makes me very happy.

In the summer there's no school. I like the summer, but I miss school. And I miss walking by the big garden every day.

9

In the fall, school starts again. It is fun to walk to school in the fall, too. The air is cool. I jump on the leaves. I love the crunchy sound of the leaves when I jump on them.

Then winter comes. I guess I love all the seasons. I love the winter, too. It is cold, but I stay warm. I wear a warm coat and hat. I wear a scarf around my neck. To keep my hands warm, I put on gloves. To keep my feet dry, I wear big boots. I like to walk in the snow. When I have time, I also like to play in the snow. I pick up some snow and make a ball. I make round snowballs, big and round. Fougere and I throw snowballs at each other. Then every-one throws snowballs. We laugh a lot.

I have lots of friends at school, and I have a nice teacher. Her name is Mrs. Collins. We learn a lot in her class. We do arithmetic. We do science experiments. They are really fun. We do a lot of English, too. English is my favorite subject. We read stories, lots of stories. We write our own stories. We read plays, and we act them out. We keep a journal, and we write down our thoughts in the journal. We can share our thoughts with the class if we want to.

Marcia shared her journal with us one day. She said she was going to take a trip to Brazil with her parents and grandparents. She is very excited about her trip. Marcia has lived in the United States for three years. She is going to visit some other people in her family. She has lots of aunts, uncles, and cousins in Brazil.

Then Kumiko started to cry. "What's the matter, Kumiko?" Mrs. Collins asked.

"I miss my father," Kumiko said. "He lives in Japan. Next year he will come to live with us, but I miss him."

"Who do you live with now?" asked Miguel. He looked very sad for Kumiko.

"I live with my mother, my brother, and my sister. We all live with my grandparents," said Kumiko.

"I live with my grandparents, too," said Marcia. "I love them a lot!" Kumiko stopped crying. She smiled a very little smile at Marcia.

"I love my grandparents, too, " said Fougere. "But they live in Haiti. I know they love me, too. They always tell me how much they miss me. And I miss them."

"When do you see them?" asked Kumiko.

"I talk to them on the phone," Fougere answered, "but next month they are going to visit us. I can't wait!"

Soon everyone was talking about their grandparents. It was fun. Everyone shared family stories. Mrs. Collins said that we were all very lucky to have grandparents. They are very special to us.

I looked at Kumiko and started to smile. Marcia, Miguel, Kumiko, and Fougere were smiling, too. Big smiles.

At the end of every day Mrs. Collins tells us to eat right and sleep well. She wants us to be "bright and chipper" in the morning. "Goodbye," Mrs. Collins says to the class.

Goodbye

"Goodbye, Mrs. Collins," we say to her. We wave to her, and we leave all together. Before we leave school, we play on the playground for a few minutes. We always have a lot to talk about.

After school, I do not go straight home. I go to my grand-parents' place. They own a hair salon. It is close to school and close to my house. It is fun to be there.

When I come in, I get a big greeting from my grandfather as he is cutting someone's hair. "Hello, there," he says in a loud voice. "How's my little school girl?"

"Just great, Grandpa!" I reply, and I give him a big hug. He laughs.

Then I run to the back of the hair salon. There is a small kitchen there. My grandmother is there. She gives me a big hug, too. Then she gives me something to eat. "Ah, Grandma, it smells and tastes so good. You're such a good cook!"

After I eat, I leave the kitchen and go to watch my grand-father. I like to get up on an empty chair. Sometimes I put both hands on the counter of front of me. I push re-ally hard and begin to spin. To go faster, I push again, and I spin around and around. When I jump off the chair, I'm really dizzy, but I run and slide across the floor. Usually my grandfather's assistant stops me with a laugh and gives me a broom. "Will you help us?" she asks. "The floor is covered with hair."

"Sure," I reply, and I sweep the floor. It is fun. I sweep all the hair into one big pile. Brown hair, black hair, red hair, white hair, and blond hair are all mixed together.

After a while, I hear my grandmother calling me. "I have to work at the cash register now," she says. "Will you help me?" I love the cash register. "Oh, wow!" I shout. My grandmother laughs. I like the sounds it makes when I push buttons and the drawer pops open. "R-R-R-Ring!" When a customer pays, I practice making change. My grandmother stands beside me as I practice. She makes sure I don't make a mistake.

My grandparents' customers are very nice. I know many of them by name. Mrs. Kramer comes to the hair salon every Wednesday. "Hi, Mrs. Kramer," I say. "Hello Olga," says Mrs. Kramer. Then she says quietly to my grandfather, "Your Olga is a nice girl. She is very polite." Grandpa gives me a big smile and a wink. I like Mrs. Kramer. She is very nice.

My grandparents work very hard. They are on their feet all day. One day grandma plopped down in a chair and took her shoes off. I plopped down right next to her. I wanted her to relax. "Let's read a book together, grandma. I have a really good book. I 'll read some pages, and then you read some pages. OK?" I said.

As I said that, I saw my grandmother lower her head and look down at the floor. "What's wrong, Grandma?" I asked.

"I don't know how to read," she said softly.

I was surprised. "What did you say?" I asked, with a puzzled look. I didn't understand.

She looked at me straight in the eye and said, "I never learned to read and write, Olga. When I was young, Russia wasn't peaceful. I couldn't go to school. It was too dangerous. When there was peace, it was too late for me to learn." There was silence for a moment. I just looked back into my grandmother's sad, blue eyes. She slowly turned her head away. I knew she was very sad. I didn't want her to be sad.

"That's OK, grandma," I said. "Don't worry. We can do something else, something together." As I said that, I felt myself sitting up tall and straight. "Yeah," I thought, "that's what we'll do — something else, together."

Grandma just looked at me. Slowly, very slowly, she smiled. My grandmother has a very pretty smile.

"Would you like me to tell you a story?" she asked.

"A story? What kind of story?" I asked.

"A true story," she said. "Just listen . . ."

I listened, and she told me a wonderful story about a time long ago when she was young. It was like a story from a book.

On many afternoons from then on, I heard stories about her and my grandfather growing up in Russia. I love it when my grandmother tells me stories. When she speaks, I can picture the people and the places in my mind.

Sometimes Grandma cooks as she tells me a story. The smell of stuffed cabbage fills the house. "Do you want a taste?" she asks. She gives me a spoonful. "Delicious!" I say, and it always is.

One day in school, Mrs. Collins said we were going to have a party. She asked us to bring in some food from home. The food would be from our own cultural background. We would share our food with each other. The whole class was excited.

"What a great idea," Marcia said.

"I'm hungry just thinking about it," said Fougere.

"I love to eat," said Miguel.

The next day Miguel brought in a Mexican bean dish that his mother had made. Kumiko brought in sukiyaki that her grandmother had made. Fougere brought in a Haitian soup that his aunt had made. Marcia brought in Brazilian feijoada that her mother had made, and I brought in latkas that my grandmother had made. They were delicious! All the food was so good.

"I'm stuffed," said Miguel. "I can't eat any more." We were all feeling a little stuffed. So for the rest of the afternoon we shared stories. It was a wonderful party.

As we all said goodbye to Mrs. Collins after the party, she said, "Sleep well tonight, I want you to be bright and chipper in the morning. Thank you all for bringing the delicious food for our party."

I was the last to leave. Mrs. Collins said, "Olga, please, thank your grandmother for us. Her latkas were really wonderful. She is a very good cook!"

As I started home, I thought about my grandparents. I thought about how I enjoy spending time with them. I thought about how they always find time to spend with me. I also thought about my grandma cooking latkas for my whole class and how she always does special things for me. I walked faster, and then faster, and then I ran.

I ran most of the way to my grandparents' place.

"Where's grandma?" I said as I ran into the hair salon.

"Not even a hello for me?" said my grandfather.

"Whoops! Sorry, Grandpa," I said, and I took a few steps backward and gave him a kiss.

Then I ran to the kitchen. There was my grandmother, ready to give me something to eat.

She said, "Oh, Olga, you look so hot and sweaty. Sit down and have a cool drink."

2 questions

I was out of breath, too, and as I sat down, I said, "Grandma, (puff puff) you always do so much for me (puff puff)." I stopped to catch my breath, and then I said, "Now I want to do something special for you. I'm going to teach you how to read and write English."

There was a long silence. Then grandma smiled the biggest smile I had ever seen! "When do we begin?" she asked.

We started that day. My grandmother was very serious.
She worked very hard. Every day after school, we worked
on reading and writing.

First, I taught her how to write her name in English:
A-L-E-X-A-N-D-R-A.

Then we wrote signs on everything in the house:
CHAIR TABLE WALL WINDOW

She wrote very slowly and carefully, practicing the letters
and saying the words. "You are a good teacher, Olga, " she
said. It was fun.

Then the next day we looked at pictures and labeled them.

We looked at lots of pictures day after day. And every day my grandmother learned more and more words. Soon her words became sentences. The sentences became paragraphs.

Next, very slowly and carefully, Grandma wrote a letter in English to her sister in Chicago. After that she wrote one of her stories, and this one was about me.

My grandfather watched her. "Olga, you are a good teacher," he said. "And your grandmother is a very good student!" We all laughed.

At last Grandma was ready. "Now it's time for books!
You can read to me, Grandma. We can read together!"
We plopped ourselves down next to each other. I snuggled
close to her, and we began to read one of my favorite books.
I helped her with the difficult words.

Near the end of the school year, Mrs. Collins said, "Next week is open school week. You can each have members of your family come to school and watch what we do in the classroom. We will make our classroom look very nice for them. Will you help me?" We were excited.

Mrs. Collins always liked to display our work. Everyone had something up on the walls. There were many stories and drawings. We had lots of books around the room. We had our science experiments out on a table. And we had our hamsters, Freddy and Neddy.

Every day different parents, grandparents, aunts and uncles came to our classroom. On Monday, Marcia came with both her grandparents. On Tuesday, Kumiko came with her mother. Fougere came with his parents on Wednesday. On Thursday, Miguel came with his aunt and uncle. My grandmother came with me on Friday.

Every day Mrs. Collins welcomed the visitors to our class. "I'm very proud of your children," Mrs. Collins said. "Please walk around the classroom and look at the wonderful work they have done."

After Mrs. Collins spoke to the visitors, my grandmother walked slowly around the room. She looked at all the work carefully. Then she stopped. She was standing in front of a story that I had written. It was really one of her stories. It was about her and my grandfather and about Russia long ago when they were young. I knew she was reading it because her lips moved as she read each word. When she was done, she smiled that wonderful smile of hers. She looked at me as tears of joy filled her eyes, and our eyes met. I smiled a very big, big smile.

Grandparents are very special people.